THE BIG(ISH) BOOK OF (SOMEWHAT) HILARIOUS POEMS

by Rich Harris and Mike Harrison

Copyright © Harris and Harrison 2017

All rights reserved.

Printed through sustainable practices, certified by:
- Forest Stewardship Council® (FSC®), Certificate Registration Code: RA-COC-004900 FSC-C084699
- Sustainable Forestry Initiative® (SFI®) Certificate Number: PwCSFICOC-345 SFI-00980
- Programme for the Endorsement of Forest Certification™ (PEFC™)

A Giant Step

Fifteen feet above the ground a giants eyes are wide
But not with anger, not at all, in fact, he's petrified

A little girl once shouted up to ask him of his fear
He shouted back "I can't stand heights, please, get me down from here!"

The little girl just laughed and said "please tell me you're not serious?"
The giant tried to nod but ended up feeling delirious

He grabbed a tree for balance and he reached out for a tower
They both came crashing to the ground, he didn't know his power

"Careful!" screamed the little girl, "you'll kill us don't you know!
I'll help as much as I am able; we'll have to take this slow."

The little girl thought long and hard and came up with a plan,
She'd try out hypnotherapy on this very peculiar man

She sat him down and waved her hands slowly at first, then fast
Within a minute it had worked, the giant was in a trance

She then began to tell him all the reasons not to fear
That being tall was really cool, so he shouldn't shed a tear

Within a week the giant was as happy as can be
Fifteen feet into the sky and always full of glee

That little girl was happy but she didn't end up smug
The giant trod on her one day and squashed her like a bug.

THE FRIENDLY ALIEN

The Friendly Alien

An alien visited us from space, to walk among the human race
He had no friends up there and only, wanted a way to not feel lonely
He parked his spaceship and then alighted to seek out friends, he felt excited;
Friends with whom he could laugh and play and giggle about silly things all day

He walked along the busy street, his five heads nodding and his pointy feet
And when his seven mouths all smiled he felt so joyful, like a child
He waddled along, this man from space, and tried to offer his embrace
But when the humans saw him coming they screamed in fear and started running

"An alien!" they shrieked in vain, "he's come to feast upon our brains;
he's strange and green and looks disgusting, I don't feel safe and I don't trust him!"
The busy streets they soon deflated, and no matter how long the alien waited
They had all gone, no one remained, his nine eyes wept, his four hearts pained

This friendly alien had been cheated, still without friendship he felt defeated
His strange existence fraught with strife; banished to space with no signs of life
He looked at his spaceship with four heavy hearts and willed his strange feet to assume their depart
His life now dictated, his misery booked, shunned by us all for the way that he looked

As he slowly turned to go he heard a small voice say hello
And there before him smiling gaily was a little girl, her name was Hayley
She looked him up and down, un-phased, the alien stared back quite amazed
Expecting her to run away, but Hayley was right there to stay

"My name is Hayley; I'll be your friend, if you don't understand then just pretend
I like your green skin, it's kind of funny, and you've sixteen noses – each one is runny!
Come on, let's go – do you like cake? I made some earlier, I love to bake!
And after cake we'll both have tea – we'll have good fun both you and me!

The alien smiled so unexpected, despite his looks he'd been accepted
Relief and happiness soon exuded, no longer was this chap excluded
Hayley showed the human touch, this pleased the alien very much
And so he entered his rebirth, and finally found a friend on earth

In life not everyone looks the same, no one's at fault and there's no blame
Be nice to people whom you meet, despite their five heads or pointy feet
Treat others how you'd treat yourself, you'll be rich with friends in untold wealth
It matters not about ones features; we are each of us friendly, loving creatures

A Fruitful Tale

Here's the story of greedy Kelly, she grew a fruit tree in her belly
One of those momentary blips, she scoffs all fruit, including pips

Her mother told her "Kelly, stop", and father yelled "Your tummy will pop!"
But Kelly just wanted to eat, she wasn't even half replete

After a while her tummy bulged, clearly she over-indulged
And from a seed, well something grows – so branches sprouted from her nose

It wasn't only branches, no, all of a sudden from head to toe
A sight so rare it begs belief but from her head out popped a leaf

Later on her fingers twitched, her arms went red and also itched
And where her hands once took their place, bananas grew at a rapid pace

Her legs they both went red and blotchy, and around her knees they too went splotchy
Her toes went POP, her feet went blue and from her ankles apples grew

This tale is getting hard to grapple, her bottom turned to a pineapple
Her ears fell off and there in drapes, each side of her head was a bunch of grapes

I think the lesson here is plain, when eating fruits try to refrain
There is no lasting happy ballad; Kelly is now a big fruit salad.

A Sick Poem

Little Bill was feeling ill, he'd felt that way for days
He really didn't know what he should do
He drank some water, rested up, splashed water on his face
But had this overwhelming need to spew

When his mother checked on him she really got a shock
The poor old woman thought it was a trick
Sadly though it wasn't so and barely had she knocked
When Little Bill covered her with sick

His Father came to visit him and see just what was wrong
'He's seems ok' the words from his mouth fell
That wasn't true, what a to do, when Little Billy belched
Father got covered in sick as well

For days Bill puked, and purged and wretched, and many times he chundered
The sick was pouring out of him so quickly
Everyone was worried and at times they often wondered
How a little boy could end up very sickly

Had he eaten something bad, had he caught a bug
Maybe he was having a reaction
To stop the sick they acted quick and took a rubber plug
And stuffed it in his mouth for satisfaction

The plug idea just didn't work; Bill groaned and looked quite odd
His parents asked him just what was the matter
Until they realised Little Bill was filling up with sick
They knew this because he was getting fatter

Out of the blue Bill brightened up, he didn't feel so bad
It seemed his sickness had finally gone
He still felt bad for being ill and puking on his family
But his happiness it didn't last too long

His mother groaned, his father moaned, his little sister cried
They clutched their bellies, looking rather queasy
Suddenly all the three of them opened their mouths wide
Little Bill, again, felt quite uneasy

Just as he thought, the bug they'd caught, all three feeling quite bad
Little Bill he shuddered, feeling grim
His lesson learned, for each in turn, one by one by one
Each took turns to now be sick on him

Albert the Astronaut

Ever since Albert was just a small child
Something he dreamed of, well it got him quite wild
His smile grew so huge and his eyes widened up, as he
Dreamed of a day when he soared through the galaxy

He wanted to be an astronaut, its true
With a space helmet silver and a shiny suit, blue
His arms would hold laser-guns, sewn to the pockets
And he would glide through the stratosphere in a really cool rocket

The only thing that seemed to leave his plans marred
Was that becoming an astronaut was really quite hard
His friends they would giggle and call him a fool
So he'd "best get his head straight and work hard at school!"

Albert was worried, what if they were right?
What if he would never ascend into flight?
But he didn't get down or succumb to their doubt
He should persevere, stay strong and see this thing out

So he set to work showing he could do hard graft
And emerged in a week with a super space-craft
Ok, there's no engine and it won't make a sound
But there are leg holes underneath so he can walk on the ground

And his laser aren't deadly, they won't pose a threat
In fact they are water-filled, you'd only get wet
And the aliens he shoots at are really not there
But for Astronaut Albert, he just doesn't care

For he is an astronaut, a galaxy defender
(But it's just in his head, he's the ultimate pretender)
And yes he works hard and achieved well at school
But his rocket and lasers proclaim he showed them all.

Dear Old Elsie

Elsie's a doll; we do have to mention her
She's 103; she's an old aged pensioner
But do not be fooled by her wizened facade
She's a sprightly old thing, a proper trump card

Now most OAP's spend their twilights in bed
Resting their old bones, laying their heads
But oh no, not Elsie – not sure what I mean?
There she is, bouncing high on that huge trampoline

When she's not bouncing, she's not sitting still
And while other OAP's moan and whinge at their will
Elsie goes food shopping, happy and jolly
She's like Formula 1, zooming around in the trolley

Shopping aside Elsie does have a passion
She's a stickler for clothing and much adores fashion
Her most favourite outfit is not brown or beige
It's a lurid pink cat-suit which she thinks is the rage

No children, no grandkids, but she doesn't moan
She never feels left out or sad or alone
Some oldies stay home - is that all they deserve?
Elsie break-dances, paintballs and is an army reserve

Well, just before Elsie at last passed away
She was quoted by someone who did hear her say
With a smile and a smirk and a bemused expression
That whenever she went, she would leave an impression

Her parting from this world inevitably did hang
And when dear Elsie went, it sure was with a bang
At the service, the mourners all let out such a titter
As her coffin blew up in swathed with fireworks and glitter

Amelia Joy Simpington Hatchcock the Third

This poem I share is quite a mad tale
In fact, it is rather absurd
'Tis about a friend who went to my school –
Amelia-Joy Simpington Hatchcock the Third

My other friends had quite simple names;
Penny, Jon, Bill, Charles and Jade
But right in the middle of our large friendship group
Was this girl with her own personal maid

She wasn't as bad as you may well be thinking
She was funny, sweet and quite tame
The only thing bad was her terrible temper
If you dared call her by the wrong name

Our friend, she would stamp both of her feet
When someone made a mistake
"It's not Amelia, nor Joy - it's really not hard"
"Say my name properly for goodness sake"

One day, a lorry in a hurry to Surrey
Came around the corner without any care
I gasped aloud, ran forward from the crowd
Around me the kids stopped and stared

"LOOK OUT AMELIA-JOY SIMPINGTON HATCH···"
But that was all I could shout
I was but half way through in calling her name
When she was hit with an almighty clout

I gasped with breath as she flew through the air
Like the poem – with the greatest of ease
I shut my eyes tight and clenched all my teeth
My stomach, it gave such a squeeze

But there was no scream, no thud or splatter
Of that I was greatly relieved
When I opened my eyes, with abject surprise
What I saw was quite hard to believe

Amelia-Joy Simpington Hatchcock the Third
Waved and shouted "I'm really quite fine"
For up in the air, above me was there
Sitting on a branch of quite a large pine

From that day forward, though still quite a snob
It turned out rather okay
When meeting new people she stuck out her hand
And simply said "Please, call me AJ"

Fatty Bird

There was a fatty birdie, with little fluffy wings
This fatty bird he loved to sing and tweet
But usually these birdies they are tiny little things
But fatty couldn't even see his feet

When it's time for feeding, for pecking on the ground
The other birds they eat a tiny portion
Then crashing through the gathering is fatty of the group
Scoffing all he can, his body in contortion

Meal times turn into a state, a horrible affair
Some birds they have to go without their dinner
But laughing loudly at the back is fatty of the group
No worry of this fatty getting thinner

It's gotten bad, he's got so big and flying is a chore
He cannot stay airborne for very long
While other flocks take to the skies and gracefully do soar
Fatty has to walk – it looks so wrong

But still he scoffs and eats and binges and stuffs his little beak
He steals away from others all their meals
I see it getting even worse, for now when fatty moves
The others have to push him around on wheels

This problem now has ended and with little intervention
It really did just clear up just like that
Due to fatty's stomach having limited retention
He just went POP and exploded with a splat

The Hungry Baby

Maddie and Bill from just down the road, were as happy as they could be
A baby boy, all bald and cute, was delivered at a quarter past three

The proud, doting parents did name the kid 'Chuck', how sweet he looked in his nursery
They sung him to sleep, then soft closed the door and went downstairs for a nice cup of tea

No sooner had they both descended the stairs when Chuck yelled out really quite loud
He shrieked and screamed, and moaned with pain, and for good measure he let out a howl

Maddie and Bill ran into Chuck's room, looking with abject concern
"Perhaps he's cold", "Perhaps he's hot", "and Perhaps he's having a bad turn!!"

Down the stairs, nursing poor Chuck, they went to the kitchen for warm milk
Maddie walked him around without making a sound; this child was as precious as silk

But Chuck would not settle, stay still, or behave; he was in a terrrrrrible mood
Then Bill came up with a most brilliant idea - "Perhaps the poor tyke just needs food"

Along with warm milk, Bill had mashed up some veg and tentatively held out a spoon
No sooner had he offered the food to the babe Chuck stopped crying⋯and none too soon!

With a chomp, a slurp and a great big belch, Chuck had scoffed away all of his meal
With a frown he peered down at the now empty bowl and then simply proceeded to squeal

In fear of the neighbours calling the cops, Maddie and Bill dashed about
Pulling food from the pantry, the cupboards and fridge, Chuck was famished, there was no doubt

For the next 16 hours they cooked and they baked, feeding Chuck all the food they had mustered
They started with yummy stuff; toast, cake and juice and then baked apple pie with warm custard

Soon the food had run low and still Chuck was not full, what else were they going to do?
But cook what was left before Chuck screamed again - could they really feed a child kangaroo?

Chuck ate rabbit and spatchcock, anchovies on pretzels, lentil burgers with offal and tripe,
Stuffed artichoke hearts with brain-truffle tarts - but still he would grumble and gripe

Chuck rolled 'round on the table, the size of a hippo, snatching all within reach of his mitts
Quickly downing raw pasta, liquid lard even faster, his parents were losing their wits

Then all of a sudden - the house it was quiet, the bloated child sated and still
He had finally had eaten his fill of the food, the dessert had been Maddie and Bill

Little Black Holes

When I was a kid there was something I did that made me change and alter my ways
Because sitting at school, always, as a rule I did something to fill up my days

I found schoolwork a bore, such a tiresome chore, so my secret I shall now disclose
After writing out words, (now this may sound absurd), but I coloured in all of the O's.

Every word with a zero made me feel like a hero, I attacked it with pen in my hand
'Til the O was all black, I would never look back, oh this feeling it made me feel grand

But one day I was scribbling, my pen just kept dribbling and I suppose I got carried away
As the O got much bigger, I scribbled on with vigour; I must have scribbled for most of the day

Then out of the blue, the O started to move, like a mouth that was opening wide
Like a person who's yawning, and then without warning, it told me to step on inside

I looked to the teacher, hoping the words had reached her, but she'd not heard a thing it had said
So I rested my pen, took a big breath and then slowly lowered my head

And climbed into the O, all the way I would go, ignoring the horrible stink
I wanted to turn back, 'cos inside it was all black and I was up to my knees in thick ink

It was icky, and sticky, and if I can be picky, it was a slimy, soggy old vault
Then a voice roared, "Hey kid, do you see what you did – all this mess and ink is your fault!"

Well, what a to do, I knew it was true and if I could've, I would have come clean
But the matter of fact is I was covered in blackness; not an inch of my skin could be seen!

I wanted to go, so I reached out of the O and started to pull myself up
But the ink made it slippy, getting out was quite tricky and I fell back into all the muck

The next thing I knew, I was free from the goo and was sitting back in my class
All the kids gathered round, no-one making a sound, until teacher decided to ask

"Where have you been, its 11:15 - you've been missing since 7 I think?
And perhaps you'll explain, without too much strain why you appear to be covered in ink!"

From then I learned that my ways must be turned, no more would I colour in O's
This may make you all laugh, but I can no longer bath – but only be washed down by hose

Marvin

He tried it for hours, consulting the manual
Wondering where it went pear shaped
'See diagram 1; 'The Shape of ones Web'
Marvin's didn't look right: his was square-shaped!

And another concern with the 'lack' of his web
Was the fact that weren't many strands
'It's not my fault' he said, 'I'm just too many legs -
All I need is just one pair of hands!'

For hours and days he tried all that he could
To perfect his style and design
A right angle here and another one there
This was going to take him some time

Night time did fall and he needed to sleep
But his web wasn't even half finished
So he slept on the floor for a few nights or more
His enthusiasm never diminished

Then early one morning he had an idea
He didn't know where to begin
It wasn't quite kosher, but he'd seen in a brochure
A house made of metal and tin

He borrowed from friends, and pilfered from neighbours
The bits that they no longer needed
And built to perfection a splendid erection
That all of his plans had exceeded

Marvin sits proudly inside his new house,
Laughing off how got in a tether
So his house wasn't quite how a web ought to be
But he's comfy, whatever the weather.

Meanie Genie

This story is about young Bert, this story is no joke
Bert rubbed a lamp upon his shirt; it caused a cloud of smoke
Bert stood back in shocked affair; the lamp fell to the floor
A Genie rose into the air while Bert looked on in awe

"Ow, my back!" the Genie moaned, the lamp had been too small
"It's not easy being stuck in there if you're over six foot tall"
"Um.." Bert said, his face went red, he felt somewhat suspicious
"Sorry sir, but can I bring up the issue of my three wishes?"

The Genie sighed, and then replied, "Oh yes, your wishes three,
They're yours of course, but with remorse for them you must pay me"
"You what?" said Bert with disbelief, "I have to give you money?
Is this a joke at me you poke, I don't think this too funny?"

"It's not a joke", the Genie spoke, and his tone was unforgiving
"I've been inside that lamp for years; I have to make a living"
Bert thought long and then he asked, "Ok then – what's the damage?"
Hoping that they would be cheap – three pounds; all he could manage

"Now let me see..." said the Genie "...That's five-pounds, isn't that nice?
And if you buy another one the fourth will be half price!
But I see your coins are not enough, so here's what I will do
Give me three-pounds, one wish is yours – I promise that is true".

Reluctantly Bert handed over all the coins he had
He now was sure that he was poor and feeling rather sad
But in reward he took his wish until the Genie started
"You silly boy, see how a fool and his money are soon parted?"

As the Genie stashed the cash and made attempt to leave
Bert, now hurt, became assert and summoned a reprieve
"I wish⋯" he said with all his might '⋯you get what you are due
Return to me my coins, all three, and another wishes-two!"

The wish was cast quite fair and square, the Genie now confronted
Bert had all his wishes now and knew just what he wanted
He wished for cash and luxuries, it was a real no brainer
And lastly, wished the genie firmly back in his container.

Miranda Rott

This is the tale of Miranda Rott, and whatever she wanted, Miranda got
Always taking, never told 'no', a selfish child was sure to grow

When supper time came, if Miranda was famished, food on the table instantly vanished
She ate every morsel then sat with a grin while the rest of her family grew terribly thin

On cold winter nights she would take all the covers, scooping up pillows and quilts from the others
How they all shivered and how they all froze while Miranda was wrapped up from head to her toes

She got the bests presents of that there's no doubt, her friends and her siblings sometimes went without
Miranda got everything, or that's what she thought but an important lesson was about to be taught

When supper time came round her mother said "Wait!", and kept all the food far from Miranda's plate
Miranda sat silent, her mouth in a pout for this time it was her who would go without

Hungry and cold, she crawled into her bed and really just wanted to rest her tired head
But her pillow had vanished - what would she do - she reached for the blanket but this had gone too

Christmas time came and Miranda got nothing, she felt like a turkey (but without the stuffing)
She'd learned a good lesson, this much was true, Miranda Rott finally knew what to do

The very next morning she woke nice and early, dressed up in her best and made her hair curly
Descended the stairs and then stood in the door and screamed to her family "I can't take any more!"

Miranda had proved that a real selfish brat will remain impervious and also show that
When things get too bad and become quite outrageous, just sell off their air looms and move to Las Vegas.

Number 12

If you should walk by No.12 - the house just on the end
Do not stop and please don't knock and go there with a friend

Strange things happen at No.12, they have a····.reputation
My friend went once, and disappeared, without an explanation

The postman won't deliver there, not even for a bet
Not since his hand was bitten - they don't even have a pet

The milk is always on the step, it's never taken in
Now all that milk has turned to cheese, some even have a skin

The residents of No.12 are quite a scary lot;
A gran, a mum, a dad, his son, a tarantula called Dot

If your football goes in their yard, you'd better just forget it
Cos if you knock, you'll get a shock - the mother probably ate it

Only once, when clouds were out, did I spy the neighbours
Skulking down the street intently; mother wearing live furs

Little Johnny at No.2 disappeared that day
The neighbours all bought crucifixes, to keep No.12 at bay

Heed my warning here my friend, do not stray outside
For if you were that foolish it could be the last time you are spied

If you see anyone at No.12, remember – be polite;
I wasn't and I ended up with a nasty, festering bite

The bite is sore, the bite is cursed, of that much I am sure
It moans to me throughout the night – I can't take anymore

And so to ensure I stay sane and end feeling bereft
Tonight I'll cut off my right arm and live with just the left.

Spike

Here's the story of a terror named Spike
He really is a tiresome tyke
A nastier child I cannot remember
Making the other kids flee with surrender

Spike is a bully, he thinks he is cool
In reality though he is really just cruel
Picking on anyone he doesn't like
Cares not who he fights – he's a nasty one, Spike

If you look different, Spike will be there
To point out your flaws and then laugh without care
Making you terrified, making you small
Everyone's frightened of his ridicule

When he's at school, all through the classes
He'll make fun of anyone who's wearing glasses
And when he's at lunch wherever he's sat
You'll be in his firing line if you are fat

And if you're not fat but are terribly thin
Spike will still taunt you, you just cannot win
Ginger-haired, chubby, thin, brainy or worse
You shouldn't be bullied if you are diverse

But here is a secret and maybe a cure
A bully is really himself insecure
No strength in his punch or the hate that he speaks
Spike is a bully, and a bully is weak

Realising bullies are nasty and loathsome
His friends they all left him, now Spike is quite lonesome
Bullies are cowards and guess how this ended -
It's not just on Facebook that a bully is unfriended.

Nutty Nora's Nowhere

Nutty Nora made a vow, to make a special potion
She stirred up things from slugs to strings, and made a sticky lotion
Into this mess she also put some hair from her pet cat
And also some old chewing gum, no harm in trying that

The mixture frothed all green and yuck, and bubbled away like mad
Her work this week was near complete, and this made Nora glad
Finally, with snails put in, the mixture was then blended
Into a paste that stunk of waste, her work had almost ended

A concoction that would avail, and certainly be clear
That once was taken, don't be mistaken, you sure would disappear
A vanishing cream Nora had made, and couldn't wait to try it
She gulped some down, it made her frown, but Nora sat there, quiet.

At first her toes began to go, and then her feet were going
Her shins, her knees, and her bottom too, it showed no signs of slowing
Until she was completely gone, she'd vanished – disappeared!
She would make a mint from this idea she pioneered!

So much fun our Nora had, with pranks on all around
She'd tap their shoulders, trip them up, or make a silly sound
And no-one knew what she had done, that she was now invisible
For years she played her silly tricks making everybody miserable

Inevitably the fun wore off and her friends all lost their patience
Nora's games had ended; to her none of this did make sense
And so she sat alone most days feeling so incomplete
Missing her friends, all she did now was be lonely in the street

The outcome of this trick, should make you stop and thank your stars
For you are there, your friends aware, they ALL know where you are
And so an end became our friend, there is no in between
One day in town, she was run down because she wasn't seen.

SuperMarge

Marge, she is a funny girl, her messy hair in shags of curls
With thick lens glasses on her nose, and dodgy shoes and funky clothes

Not much to look as is our Marge, kind of clumsy with feet too large
Domestic aspirations: zero, but she's desperate to be a superhero

How she wished that she could fly, soaring up into the sky
Fighting crime for hours and hours, loaded up with super powers

And if she saw a naughty man, she'd stop him fast because she can
Discharging lasers from her eyes and taking villains by surprise

And if a family needed rescue, SuperMarge would be the best to
Dash in bravely, show no fear, and free that family out of here

Your kitten up that tree is stuck? Well here comes SuperMarge, what luck!
She'll land that cat without a bump, by using her Bionic Jump

And if someone has robbed a bank, well, Marge would be the one to thank
Thwarting robbers is permissible, SuperMarge can be invisible

"Aha!" she shouts trying to bluff them, so that the police may come and cuff them
Her villain tick-list growing large, and all this thanks to SuperMarge

But a superhero she'll never be, without her glasses she just can't see
She'd never satisfy a mission with less than 20/20 vision

And then of course there are those feet that stop her running down the street
They pretty big, it's fair to say that every villain would get away

So Marge is mortal just like us and still she doesn't make a fuss
Short-sighted, big-footed, I tell no lies, Marge is still super in our eyes.

The Bed Monster

"There's a monster under my bed!" I said
"Don't be silly, it's all in your head" they said
I shook my head, "Please look!" I said
While I screwed up my eyes, and my face filled with dread

"Nope, nothing there, close your eyes" said my Pa
"And see you tomorrow, when you rise" added Ma
But I just didn't care; I was full of despair,
Contemplating that my demise may not be far.

When they left me there I thought: 'Why am I hurting?
A monster, in here, can I be more uncertain?
How silly of me, scared of things I can't see'
Then a guttural roar came from behind the curtains

"The monster!" I shrieked, but too little avail
As it swooped down onto me, while flicking its tail
Its face was contorted, its body distorted
And from horned head to talon, was covered in scales

It sat for a while, then said "My name is Keith"
And then flashed me a smile that showed too many teeth
"It's a pleasure to meet you, now I'm going to eat you"
The only thing I could say then was "Good grief!"

He took a large bite of me, showing no warning
Licking its lips at the sight of my mauling
I screamed "Why so hasty?" he said "You're too tasty;
And what I can't finish now I'll just save 'til the morning".

By 7am I was gone, nothing more
Than a couple of teeth and some bones on the floor
For my parents to find, I hoped they wouldn't mind
That I never got round to completing my chores

This story is not meant to frighten or scare
It's a way for you parents to show some more care
If your kids say they're frightened, listen up, be enlightened
Because in the morning, they may not be there.

The Do's and Don't of Dares

The stories written out below are tales of truth and woe
Each one a dare, not meant to scare…just how far will you go?

Little Mickey once dared Ricky to hold in all his farts.
Ricky took the challenge on, he couldn't wait to start.
For seven days and seven nights, into this trick he was goaded
The tragic outcome of this dare, poor Ricky soon exploded.

Little Grace was fair of face, her blonde hair long and soft
Her dare from Claire, was quite unfair, and was to shave it off.
Grace embraced a pair of clippers while others watched, enthralled,
Her hair won't grow back anymore, and little Grace is bald.

Gary dared his sister once, while playing hide and seek
That it was swell to hide down a well and never make a peep
She took the dare and then descended and never made a sound
Three days on, guess how it ended, she still hasn't been found

Lisa Turner, somewhat slow learner was dared by her friend Kate
To chew on glue, something to do and so she took the bait
She opened wide and stuffed some in, no doubt it made her frown
You won't get chatting to Lisa now, not unless she writes it down.

In London, Harry and his friend Barry, wanted so much to fly
This might sound drastic, but they took some elastic and to a tree it was tied
The other end was tied to each friend and pulled hard to create tension
They were last seen near Aberdeen, they'd flown too far to mention

So there you have it, a guide of sorts to help if you are dared
You make the choice, you have the voice – my advice is just be prepared.

The Explosive Youth Potion

Professor White stayed late each night
He had to get this potion right
And if he did, Eureka kid!
He'd surely get his name in lights

He really was a wizened chap
His body creaked, his bones might snap
This poor old guy, he really tried
For years to capture his youth back

Now other potions come and go
Some make you fast, some make you slow
But his creation, without explanation
Would really stop how old you grow

His potion was the latest craze
To keep you young and never age
Forever young for everyone
No more old biddies, only babes

He had to test that it was working
And show the world he wasn't jerking
He jabbed a marrow with a tainted arrow
And ended up with a baby gherkin

Professor White was feeling tired
In fact, his body was near expired
It was time to stop and take a drop
And shed the years that he'd acquired

Alas it ends here, that's no lie
He drank too much but didn't die
He craved his youth that is the truth
Now he's just a glint in his father's eye.

The Last Little Cupcake

A dozen cupcakes baked fresh that day, ready and waiting, all sat in their tray
All of the cupcakes were uniform and neat, except one at the back, it just looked incomplete
That last little cupcake was not the right size - its colour was off and it just didn't rise
It was smaller and paler, and tried though it might, the last little cupcake just didn't look right

The other eleven looked golden and sweet, all perfectly formed, what a wonderful treat!
When customers saw them they couldn't resist, such beautiful cakes were the top of their list
Little wonder that all of the cakes sold out fast, except for the one who'd been left until last
Make no bones about it, right down to the letter, the other cakes sold out because they looked better

Well, even though most of the cakes had been bought, a lesson unfolding was about to be taught
Suddenly people came back complaining, shouting and yelling, their anger was raining
Praise on their cupcakes now quickly redeemed, their wonderful cakes weren't all that they seemed
Some had been gooey, and some couldn't tell but the cakes had been burnt and had started to smell

"That cupcake you sold me was bitter and sour!" "The one I ate made me sick, hour after hour!"
"Well I bought a cake which was hard; broke my tooth!" "The one I had was vile and that is the truth!"
The shopkeeper scratched his head he felt confused and recounted the list of ingredients used
His cakes had looked excellent; looked like the best, even though one stood out from the uniform rest

Then right at that moment causing a stop, a lady stepped in through the door of the shop
"Oh goody! She squealed "there's a cupcake, hooray I heard they sold out but this has made my day!"
The shopkeeper panicked "Please no more, I've refunded these people please don't make me poor!
You can't have this cupcake its ugly and sad and I can't guarantee but it might taste too bad"

She pondered a moment on hearing these words, the cake did look different she should feel deterred
But she wasn't put off and devoured the cake, the others all gasped, had she made a mistake?
She chewed and chomped and eventually swallowed, the onlookers eager to see what now followed
Her eyes opened up and she shouted aloud "THAT CAKE WAS DELICIOUS" to an astonished crowd

"I quite understand why you left this cake last, but in future you really should try to see past
There's much more to life than the outer appearance, it's good to apply all and sundry adherence
It just goes to show is there is much more within, if we only look deeper and under the skin
Perhaps you are 'perfect', and 'twinkly-eyed' but that won't stop you being revolting inside."

The Prettiest Witch

Elspeth stared dreamily, at her reflection; her skin was so oily and green
To some she was ugly, but she saw perfection – the prettiest witch she had seen

Her nose was shaped wrong and was really quite long, with a big wart stuck on the end
The wart was covered in thick, wiry hairs which she permed because that was the trend

Onto her mouth she had painted a smile; a lipstick of crusty, old black
She felt really thrilled, yellow teeth were revealed, whenever her thin lips drew back

She adjusted the hat, on which her had sat, her wiry hair underneath
It was matted and knotted and smelt like it rotted – to Elspeth, this was a relief

But Elspeth was worried, she looked around hurried, the other girls pretty and thin
And with every glance she felt she had no chance of ever hoping to win

On stage they all lined up, Elspeth wondered why she signed up – she wanted to just run away
And as her face burned, slowly she turned and then heard someone shout "Hey!"

It was one of the judges who she'd thought held begrudges and before she could say she was sorry
The judge how he beamed; she was wrong it now seemed, he said to her "Hey greeny…don't worry!"

"I think you're swell, yes you do look odd, well that's okay cos that's something we seek…
…these other girls mesh – but you really impress – we think you're really unique!"

As the curtain came down, on her head was the crown, Elspeth felt really quite proud
In this beauty test she outshone the rest all because she stood out from the crowd.

The Well-mannered Ogre

Most ogres live in filth and muck
Most ogres love their slime
Most ogres though are not like James
'Cos James is rather fine

His vacuum cleaner is always on
And he's always, always cleaning
You'll never find one speck of dust
In fact his house is gleaming

And James is not like other ogres
He wallows not in mud
In fact he bathes in bubble bath
Just soaking in the tub

Most ogres are quite hideous
Brown teeth, green skin, BO
Our James is not like that at all
He's such a pleasant soul

If you should knock upon his door
Don't worry, for heaven's sake
For James will welcome you right in
With tea and chocolate cake

So if you thought that ogres
Were vile and brutish thugs
Think back to James as you left his house
And how he smothered you in hugs.

The Wicked Icecream Vendor

Roll up, roll up, and get your treats here
Said the wicked ice-cream vendor, with a slight of a sneer
All kinds of flavours, so new and exciting
You must try my 'special ones', they're so inviting!

Yes we have Strawberry, and yes there's vanilla
But a 'special ingredient' I keep in my chiller
If you want to try it you just have to say
And a 'special' ice cream will be right on its way

It's not made of fruit, and it's not made of jelly
But you will get a nice feeling down in your belly
Don't mind the chewy bits, they are quite edible
Doesn't my special ice-cream taste incredible?

What do you mean you have found something bony?
Are you trying to say that I'm some kind of phoney?
So what, it's just bone, just don't give it a thought
What's the matter there sonny, you look quite distraught.

I have an idea; it's yours for the taking
You're just the right weight for a new flavour I'm making
Come on with me, I will show you the start of it
And you will end up really 'being a part of it'

No you don't want to? Well, that makes me frown
Soon my ice-cream will be all over this town
I just have to top up my special ingredient
But children these days are no longer obedient

Ok, off you go then, I have to keep trying
And I'll be ok, if the kiddies keep buying
Just keep our talk today nice and quiet
If they found out about it there would be a riot

Run along sonny, go play with the rest
And if you need an ice-cream, then come for the best
Roll up, roll up, and get your treats here
Said the wicked ice-cream vendor, with the hint of a sneer.

Too Fat to be a Fairy

The job description read 'Light and airy; that's what you need to become a true fairy',
Brenda looked solemn upon reading this and while walking away took a bite of her Twix.

All of her life she had wanted to be just like a real fairy on top of the tree
Looking down proudly for all to admire, but she wanted to do this without pulleys and wires

Diets, exercise, she tried it all but had to admit she was shaped like a ball
She even tried ladders and stood on friends shoulders, to get up that tree was like throwing a boulder

At the 'Fairy Job Centre' she just sat and listened while the thin fairy brigade took theirs orders, and glistened
Primping their fairy wings, fixing their hair, sniggering at Brenda with without any care

Brenda sat awkward, her eyes they did well up, since lunch she had eaten enough cake to swell up
She broke down and cried, it was too much to see as the other thin fairies ascended their trees

That was some years ago and Brenda's got bigger, she never did get a good grip on her figure
And as dreams of becoming a fairy had dwindled she realised an old dream could be re-kindled

She still loves her Christmases, she no longer dawdles, she found a new job; she is one of the baubles
Hanging there proudly all nice and shiny and lost in the tinsel, she is positively tiny.

Is there a moral to this little prose, who has an answer, who rightly knows?
One things for sure and it's easy to flaunt - whoever you are, you can be what you want.

The Stingiest, Wealthiest Man

Victor Sneer was a millionaire
He had bundles of money, but just didn't care
Now don't be deluded, you will not be right
Because this millionaire was incredibly tight

He rarely spends money, won't go on a spree
And will only consume foods that he finds for free
When Christmas arrives - this may fill you with doubt
But don't wait for a present – you will go without

His house is in darkness, won't turn on a light
The heating stays off – he is cold through the night
It's amazing to think and some may say 'disgusting'
But he won't spend a dime though is wallet is busting

I've pondered this question with quite persistence
But why would a man live on such an existence
Well, dear Victor Sneer is a procrastinator
He won't spend it now; he will 'save it for later'

One time it was said with immediate clarity
"Just give all your money away to a charity!
There's plenty less fortunate who are in need
Don't be such a miser, don't wallow in greed!"

But Victor declined without any relent
"If they have no money, then that's what is meant
My money is MINE, no pity, no sorrow
It's mine, mine, all mine - I might spend it tomorrow!"

Now, just as the sun broke the very next day
(By quite a coincidence I have to say)
Something had shifted and Victor declared
He would dish out his fortune; he no longer cared

"I have been quite selfish" he said with a pout
And would start throwing bundles of money about
But before he could issue a drop of his wealth
Victor dropped dead; a victim of poor health

This is the problem for those who will wait
You may miss the moment and it may be too late
The only thing that's guaranteed if you save
Is the title of 'Wealthiest Man in the Grave.'

We All Applaud Maude

This is a story, that's kind of amusing
It's a story of a woman called Maude
She was once a bee-keeper but soon turned thrill-seeker
Because she was constantly bored

After sixty-two years of life's repetition
She needed to do something new
She cashed in her giro and sold off her house
And travelled her way around Peru

A few months of travel let her life unravel
She woke every day without knowing
Her routine had shattered – this rarely mattered
She loved having nothing to do

Once back on home turf, she wanted to surf
So she upped and flew off to Australia
Life was a peach running on Bondi Beach
As a surfer though, she was a failure

'Where next?' she reckoned – then India beckoned
She would visit the Taj Mahal
But once she got there she was full of despair
She just found the whole thing quite dull

Rome was a let down, she'd seen it before
A country, its people, their faces
It was getting the same to just jump on a plane
The world was full of similar places

Maude suddenly realised her life was idealised
She needed a kind of re-birth
She would fly into the sky – you know, really quite high
And then jump out, plummeting to the earth

With the instructor explaining the rules of plane sailing
Maude started to feel a bit down
Ok – she would jump – but what gave her the hump
Was pretty soon she'd be back on the ground

When the sky-dive was done she needed more fun
Something truly fantastic
Maybe jump from a height, feeling really quite light
Suspended only by elastic

As she dropped from the sky – from 40 metres high
The onlookers watching and clapping
She looked down to her legs and then suddenly said
"Should this elastic be snapping?"

Her death was inevitable, her time was up
Pretty soon she was bound to be floored
Maude wasn't peeved – in fact, just relieved
For certain she'd no longer be bored

www.ingramcontent.com/pod-product-compliance
Lightning Source LLC
Chambersburg PA
CBHW042229010526
44113CB00046B/2930